Portrait of
EDINBURGH

First published in Great Britain in 1994 for

Lomond Books
36 West Shore Road
Granton
Edinburgh EH5 1QD

British Library Cataloguing in Publication Data
Baxter, Colin
Portrait of Edinburgh
I. Title
914.134

ISBN 0–948661–42–9

Printed in Hong Kong

Front Cover Photograph: *EDINBURGH FROM SALISBURY CRAGS*
Back Cover Photograph: *THE CITY FROM CALTON HILL*

Portrait of
EDINBURGH

PHOTOGRAPHS BY
COLIN BAXTER

TEXT BY
JIM CRUMLEY

LOMOND BOOKS
EDINBURGH • SCOTLAND

CONTENTS

A TRINITY OF HILLS

And yet the place establishes an interest in people's hearts; go where they will, they find no city of the same distinction.

- Robert Louis Stevenson, 'Picturesque Old Edinburgh'

It is not a castle, or even a royal palace, and certainly not a Parliament, which is at the heart of Edinburgh, but a trinity of hills. You need three, because two of them demand to be stared at, and as the relationship between them is crucial to any lingering appreciation of the best urban skyline in the land, you need the third one to stand on.

Robert Louis Stevenson, sublime portrayer of his native city, fingered problem and solution unerringly.

> 'Of all places for a view, this Calton Hill is perhaps the best; since you can see the Castle, which you lose from the Castle, and Arthur's Seat which you cannot see from Arthur's Seat.'

Edinburgh is what it is because its fame came down from the crown of a rock like the Ten Commandments, and because it nurtures a mountain in its midst. A mountain in a city is a curiosity, even a phenomenon. Fulmars nest on its cliffs (a remarkable accommodation, a round of ten miles for every mouthful of chick-nourishing fish), snow buntings cat-nap there on winter journeys, and short-eared owls beat their uncanny wings across its flanks. Kestrels hold up in its many winds, eyeing the tawny backs of foxes, and from the loch at its foot, skeins of greylag geese and mute swans forever punctuate the city skylines with the exclamation marks of their flights. And on days of crystalline winter clarity you can look out from the mountain's summit over improbable distances to the snowy Highland north where so many episodes of Scotland's bloody story spawned and ultimately washed up on Edinburgh's doorstep. This historic bridge between Highlands and Lowland capital is an association of realms as old as Scotland, and its far mountain profiles assist the cause of Arthur's Seat's mountain-ness. Edinburgh breathes easiest here where sea winds are compulsory. On the crystalline days it feels such a free place, but every mountain knows its dank gray days too, and then it's a mountain in a cage called Edinburgh and the city at your feet is all the world there is and you fear you'll never again imprint the snows of far Schiehallion.

But try it, too, if you have the inclination and the steadiness of nerve, at night when (as Stevenson has it) 'the town lies blue and darkling on her hills'. The mountain masses before you and blackens as you climb away from the city. There seems twice as much mountain now, its every dimension unfathomable, its every footfall uncertain. The fox, should you meet him now, goes footsure and confident and senses that you do neither, and knows briefly a supremacy over his oldest rival.

Climb as high as you dare, as deep into the mountain folds as you dare, then turn and marvel at the lit city, for the landscape of Edinburgh is such that even in the dark there is no mistaking it for any other place on the map. 'Thus,' wrote Stevenson, 'the plan of the city and her suburbs is mapped out upon the ground of blackness . . . not the darkest night of winter can conceal her high station and fanciful design; every evening in the year she proceeds to illuminate herself in honour of her own beauty . . .'

There are those who will scoff at the idea of Arthur's Seat as a mountain. Its height of 822 feet is topped by thousands of anonymous Highland cairns, but Stevenson has an answer for the scoffers: 'A hill for magnitude, a mountain in virtue of its bold design . . .' and what was good enough for Stevenson should be good enough for the rest of us. Mountain it is. The 'bold design' from a wind-deflecting niche on Calton Hill is underpinned by two slashing, climbing, red sandstone diagonals of low cliff. One - Salisbury Crags - is bolder than the other in the way it girdles the mountain shoulder like a bandoleer, in the way it climbs to its own reddening sunset prow. The other seems much more the issue of the mountain itself, gathered in by its shadowiest folds beneath its imperiously leonine summit. It would all be head-turning enough if it rose from a Highland moor. That it hallmarks a mediaeval capital city further distinguished by a castellated rock and furnished with this generous viewing stance of Calton Hill, and all of it wide open to sea and hill winds and kaleidoscopic shifts of light...that truly amounts to a store of landscape riches from which Stevenson rightly concludes that there is 'no city of the same distinction'.

From Salisbury Crag, though, Calton Hill is a low and pointless shrug with its eccentrically implanted Greek affectations and its Nelson Monument of which Stevenson (ever the shrewd judge) wrote '. . . it ranks among the vilest of men's handiworks'. The mountain is the Old Town's hill. From here you see the wondrous mediaeval confusion

THE CASTLE FROM CALTON HILL

The Calton Hill is perhaps the finest viewing stance in all
Edinburgh. Here the Castle dominates on its rock, the crowning glory
of the Old Town. The spire of the Tolbooth Highland St John Kirk, the highest
point of the Old Town skyline, is prominent on the left above the floodlit
Bank of Scotland. The Balmoral Hotel dominates the east end of
Princes Street, the Scott Monument beyond.

THE BALMORAL HOTEL AND CALTON HILL

To the people of Edinburgh it will always be 'the NB', but
one of the consequences of the restoration of the old North British Hotel
was that it changed its name to the Balmoral. Another enlightened restoration was
the North Bridge, the first link between the Old Town and what would
become the New Town. The backdrop is the National Monument
and the up-ended telescope of the Nelson Monument.

of gray stone in all its built forms, clinging to and crowding in on that wondrous simplicity of nature's gray stone, the summit of which is the Castle Rock. It is that most adaptable of nature's set pieces, a volcanic plug. You fortify the crown of it, (and Edinburgh Castle Rock has been fortified since long before it occurred to anyone to try building in stone instead of timber), and you evolve your town downhill in the lee of your fortifications, slowly over millenia. When you have finally filled the rock, crammed its every corner and spilled down its cliffs, setting your thatchers and carpenters and stonemasons to ape nature setting stone on stone, cliff on cliff, crown on crown; finally spilled beyond the containing wall you built to keep your town as well as your castle defendable, you summon a visionary genius. Edinburgh summoned a six times Lord Provost called George Drummond who dared to throw a bridge from the spine of the Old Town north across a boggy valley, and there tame woods and fields and wilderness to build a New Town. But such is the distinction of this Edinburgh that even its New Town would be celebrated in lesser cities for its antiquity.

From the Mountain, the New Town is nothing but a misted hint, but from the Rock, from the Castle walls, you get something of the sense of it. You see a place of order and greenery and you wonder at the nature of the man who could dream up such a thing from the introverting dilapidation of the Old Town, which by the 18th century was as raucous and reeking as a Bass Rock gannetry in June. The Castle Rock commands. You see at once why it became what it has become. You make sense of Drummond's vision and you see why it was necessary. You see the singular street of the Old Town, the Royal Mile, set off giddily downhill, a stone river, hell-bent on its destination, the Palace of Holyroodhouse. You see too how Arthur's Seat and Calton Hill stand, unequal gateposts, through which Scotland's destiny has long been accustomed to march. But then you look around you at the embrace of battlement and battery, at the might of stronghold, the gleam of crown, the sanctity of chapel, and you realise that you don't climb to the Castle for the view.

So it is, of all Edinburgh's lofty stances, Calton Hill which offers the truest perspective. It lays out the mediaeval city in its true origins between Rock and Mountain. It spins Princes Street below your feet like the central strand of a new web and (despite the unflattering bulwark of New St Andrew's House and the St James Centre which out-vile by far the modest atrocity of the Nelson Monument) brings the New Town into sharper focus, over your right shoulder. Stubborn, seagoing Leith is far over to your left.

But what are you to make of the rash of silly Greek things which bestrew the place? The National Monument to the fallen of the Napoleonic Wars, built to look Greek and abandoned half-way, built to look ancient and looking only askance at itself, a theatre set which most of the audience turn their backs on because the great theatre of Edinburgh lies elsewhere; temples to the great and the good, including one to Burns . . . a temple for a ploughboy - strange; one to Playfair who built the observatory nearby and the National Gallery of Scotland and Royal Scottish Academy in Princes Street - Greek-ish all of them, so perhaps he merits his temple. Perhaps Edinburgh merits its little show of eccentricity too, for it's too often misportrayed by outsiders as a dour gray place. But the soubriquet of 'The Athens of the North' which the Victorians conferred upon it is a preposterous claim, wryly put down by its own inhabitants who turn their collars to the sea wind and mutter darkly about Reykjavik of the South. Edinburgh has a sense of humour too.

So you go down from this curious hilltop fantasy in sandstone with your eye on the mediaeval hub of the city, and you go eagerly down to the stony labyrinth, curiously down through the shadows to its lowest rock-bottom gesture, and you find not a darkly cramping dungeon but a royal palace enthroned in its own spaciousness and boldly supporting the tremulous decay of its own abbey. The site is the perfect fulcrum between the Mountain which overwhelms its southern aspect and the Rock which trails upwards and westwards away from this its lowest ebb. The composer Mendelssohn memorably wrote:

> In the twilight today we went to the Palace where Queen Mary lived and loved. . . . the chapel beside it has now lost its roof, it is overgrown with grass and ivy, and at the broken altar, Mary was crowned Queen of Scotland. Everything is ruined, decayed and open to the sky. I believe I have found here today the beginning of my Scotch Symphony.

For lesser mortals than Mendelssohn there can be other beginnings. The Palace of Holyroodhouse is the place to start any exploration of the Old Town. The site is where the first settlers from the sea would begin, and uphill is the way of all the Royal Mile's countless great processions. And besides, the architecture of nature demands it.

ARTHUR'S SEAT AND SALISBURY CRAGS

THE CASTLE AND ARTHUR'S SEAT
Summer evening sunlight catches the west face of the Castle
and the roofs of the Old Town while the shadowy bulk of Edinburgh's
own mountain, Arthur's Seat, creates the perfect setting. The relationship
between the mountain and the Castle on its rock is one of the
chief delights of the Edinburgh landscape.

THE OLD TOWN AND NORTH BRIDGE

THE BALMORAL AND THE CASTLE

The striking contrast of one architectural form against another
is a recurring theme in Edinburgh. Here the Balmoral Hotel breaks
the skyline of the Castle. Opposite: The lower viewpoint and dramatically
different light throw the famous clock tower against a dusky sky
while Princes Street goes about its business below.

SOUTH SIDE, THE MEADOWS AND MARCHMONT

THE BANK OF SCOTLAND

The green-domed Bank of Scotland building on the Mound
is one of the most striking late additions to the cliff-perching north
face of the Old Town. This high viewpoint also shows the depth of the
valley between the Old Town and the New Town which the
North Bridge had to cross.

SUNSET OVER THE CASTLE

The path of the sun round the Castle Rock is forever
working a sorcerer's repertoire of lighting tricks. One of the
most impressive is a spring sunset when the sun goes down behind
the Castle's silhouette and the Old Town's east-facing
shape is in unfathomable shadow.

RAMSAY GARDEN IN SUMMER

THE OLD TOWN

From any distant vantage point, the Old Town is a skyline. Quite apart from the climactic Castle it marches erratically uphill in a frozen tumult of garrets and high gables, regiments of chimney blocks, spires and towers and turrets, and holding the whole thing together like a good hinge, the ancient see-through crown of St Giles. It is the skyline of that singular thoroughfare from Palace to Castle, the Royal Mile, first avenue of Scotland's story.

In its gray midst, the Royal Mile remains a brave and impressive place. There are few places in any city in the land where the sense of stepping in history's sod is quite so tangible, where there is such an aura of destiny. This singular street has been a stupendous stage for many of Scotland's dramas, and almost all the stars of her history. That old aura is an omnipresence, veined with sleights of hand and subtleties of mood and character which dilute and intensify it by turns. Whatever the magic and malevolence of such moods, however, they rely for their effect on the stage they play. It is first a crammed place, heaped with built stone, a tumbling riverbed of gray setts from which the stone-flagged tributaries of the closes spill and slither. The closes, an instinctive rhythmic solution of centuries of stonemasons, also bring a sense of ragged order to nature's chaotic ground rules for building a city on such a rock. They tunnel deepest into the weave of the Old Town fabric, offer furtive glimpses of its old stone soul, and still have the capacity to surprise leisured strollers and astound hardened historians not easy to impress, by revealing new fragments of their oldness. It is a phenomenon of this simplicity of design (the tributaries flowing north and south from a parent river flowing west to east) that the juxtaposition of the two can create adjacent and opposite miniature climates of light and shade, storm and sanctuary.

The second characteristic of the Royal Mile as a stage, is that it is a high and windy place, so that the light and the air are seldom still. The closes offer not just tunnels but funnels, not just windtraps but windbreaks, not just stone burrows but sunshafts and shadowshafts, counteractions and contradictions. They weave a rich tapestry. They also offer brief immunity from that clammy cape of sea fog, the haar, the city sometimes swirls about its own shoulders. It is that phenomenon, the haar, which most displeases

Edinburgh's weather-weary citizenry, a miles-wide cocoon of restless, airy ooze which severs the Castle from its rock and rolls among the crowsteps and shines the setts and seeps gray ice into a human heart. Yet step out into the Royal Mile swaddled in such a wet blanket, and it becomes again the whole city and you begin to grasp the significance of where you stand, in the old stone embrace of a city which invented its New Town more than 200 years ago. But now, if you would explore oldest Edinburgh, the Palace of Holyroodhouse is your best beginning.

Holyrood remains Mary's. No figure in the Edinburgh of any era better personifies that 'exquisite agony' than Mary Queen of Scots. No-one won more hearts and more enemies. Yet for all the heroes and villains who followed her, for all the kings and would-be kings and conquerors, all their masons and architects and artists who nurtured their whims Holyrood has never relinquished the exquisitely sorrowing pervasiveness of Mary's spirit. Her apartments remain an aloof sanctuary for the spirit of her life and times. They are unregally cramped and attended by an intangible presence which not even the prosaic delivery of a Palace guide dispels. She dug the heels of her Catholicism into the Edinburgh of John Knox's stern and outraged Presbyterianism. She threw her flame-haired glances on the crass and fushionless Darnley when she might have had any lord in the land. When she turned to the flattering intellectual, Riccio, her jealous court feared a Papist mole and put a brutal end to his glamorous (and probably platonic) association with his queen. There are countless episodes of royal history walled into the 17th-century Holyrood Palace which took as its architectural starting point the simple tower house that was Mary's. Royal history is made there still, and although the Abbey no longer offers sanctuary to criminals and commoners as it once did (in an era when the theft of a loaf or failure to notify a pregnancy were hanging offences), there is contemplative sanctuary of a kind in its mesmeric ruin. It may not stir a symphony in you, but it is a dull soul which is not moved there to an appreciation of the historic significance of where it stands.

The Canongate beckons, establishing an architectural mood, a canyon in stone, which prevails more or less unbroken all the way to the Castle. Its sense of unity disguises the hands of many eras, for mostly the mediaeval spirit of the street has been honoured. But Scots is not the only architectural tongue you hear in the Canongate. Step aside into White Horse Close (it is an addiction, this stepping aside into the Old Town's teeming

WHITE HORSE CLOSE
The cool Dutch architecture of this beautiful Canongate
courtyard is a 1962 restoration of the White Horse Inn, built in 1623.
An orderly calm now pervades but 17th-century illustrations
depict the inn as a bustling, even raucous place.

HOUSE WALL, CANONGATE

Old stone was worked in countless different ways through the
different eras of the Old Town. The oldest of it is rubble-built like this
beautifully lit wall near the Tolbooth. Many a close mouth was embellished by
stone carvings, although not all are as elaborate as this one. Stonemasons
often exacted revenge against a hated boss or difficult client in the
carved faces. After all, once it was up, what could you do?

repertoire of closes) and find an impeccably restored fragment of Holland washed up by an old tide of trade which ebbed and flowed across the North Sea, which marked its passage in the architecture of the east coast, especially the Forth shores of Fife and East Lothian. Set its brilliant whitewash and pantile figure against the dark-timbered Scottish understatement of Bakehouse Close across the street and people the whole thing in your mind with a teeming cosmopolitan bustle of trade and tongues and drama and drunks, the buildings more roughed-up than restored.

Much of the more enlightened of the Royal Mile's restoration is the work, directly or indirectly, of two men, Patrick Geddes and Robert Hurd. Geddes won the epitaph of 'the father of town planning' for his timely recognition at the turn of the century of the worth of his surroundings, an appraisal of how much still survived and how far that survival was at risk. Hurd was an architect who practised what he preached: that the Scottish tradition was a force with a future as well as a past, and that people, particularly Scots, responded to it with an instinctive warmth. He brought his philosophy to bear on telling restorations and crucial patchwork darning in the fabric of the Old Town.

His Canongate restoration of the braggart gusto of Huntly House is typical. The Royal Mile is host to several mansions, mostly discreeter than this, but their sadness is that they are - none of them - lived in. For all the sense of continuity through earlier eras which the Canongate imparts, much has changed irrevocably in the street's way of life.

For all the Old Town's dalliances with the Lord and his infinite manifestations in built stone, only the Canongate's kirkyard survives, carefully tending its congregation of celebrated souls. Chief among them is George Drummond, Lord Provost extraordinary (six times between 1725 and 1760). His claims to fame are astonishing for one man in one city. He was the champion of the university and the instigator of the Royal Infirmary, friend of Hanoverian kings and foe of Jacobites to the extent of mustering his own farcical and quite abortive defence of the city against Bonnie Prince Charlie in 1745. He chose his civic campaigns with better judgement.

He is remembered as the father of the New Town, daring to dream a new and purpose-built Edinburgh elegance far beyond the squalor of the Old Town's swarming rock-thirled confines. Although he died before the New Town was built he inspired the leap of thought which flung the North Bridge out from the Old Town to what is now Princes Street. Then it was the far shore of an unsavoury loch and bog. That single stroke

ANCHOR CLOSE, HIGH STREET

of genius unlocked the whole New Town enterprise and his spirit is still invoked whenever Edinburgh drags its heels in civic endeavour.

Then there is Robert Fergusson, Old Town poet, who died young and was buried in a pauper's grave, only to achieve immortality of a kind at the hands of the poet he influenced most, one Robert Burns. Burns had him buried here, with a stone which bears these words:

Here lies Robert Fergusson, poet.
Born September 5, 1751, died October 16, 1774

No sculptured Marble here nor pompous lay
No storied Urn nor animated Bust
This simple stone directs Pale Scotia's way
To pour her sorrows o'er her Poet's Dust

Alas Pale Scotia has saved her sorrowing for other causes and Fergusson remains neglected and unsung. His street-wise poetry was the root from which Burns blossomed, and his language is a Scots with authentic vitality which today's few marginalised Lallans poets can never reinvent. He wrote a piece of exquisite vitriol against the Tron Kirk Bell; he was obviously over familiar with it:

If magistrates wi me wud 'gree
For ay tongue-tackit shud you be,
Nor fleg wi antimelody
Sic honest folk,
Whase lugs were never made to dree
Thy dolefu' shock.

The ghost of a gate once barred the Royal Mile here. What it barred the Canongate folk from was Edinburgh, for the Canongate was its own burgh. When you step through the Netherbow port you are in the High Street, Edinburgh, and although the city has long since usurped the Canongate and its older burgh status, something indefinable has been left behind. Edinburgh was in no doubt of the distinction, for the first close you encounter in the High Street is called World's End, the name signifying an assessment of what lay beyond - the Canongate in other words. The feeling was more or less mutual once, but it was Edinburgh which took the trouble of nailing it to the wall.

John Knox wouldn't have liked this! Idolatrous hordes of pointed fingers and camera lenses! Favourite haunt of the open-topped buses! A shrine! The most charismatic house in town, and it's *his*. Or is it? John Knox's House juts tenaciously out into the street, like a good chin. Even if he were here it wasn't for long, yet this Royal Mile mansion house is saddled with his name, and like the rest it is not lived in, but a museum. Moubray House next door is lived in, and although discreeter by far, it is just as old, and five hundred years of continuous habitation have put a different kind of stamp on it, a warmer one. I look at Knox's House and I think 'Why can't it be lived in?' but like everybody else, I look at it and admire it too, every time I pass. It is one fragment of old Edinburgh Mary might recognise if she saw it now.

The Old Town clambers on up its hill, cloaking itself in restorations and facades, burrowing down the tributaries of the closes, sometimes to hidden courtyards, once to an unheralded and startlingly pretty replica 17th-century garden, often to decrepit disappointment or fragments of barely believable oldness.

In the midst of it stands a brave new building, a hotel which dares to hark back to the street's mediaeval heyday, combining elements of tower house and towering tenement, in its timber and stone detailing and slate and pantile roofs, and bold colour-washed harled walls. It works because of its scale and its sense of place, although it has been derided by some with the all-purpose architectural put down - 'pastiche'. What it is, is Scottish. It is the work of Ian Begg, and carries the perfect pedigree for the street, for the young Ian Begg learned from the horse's mouth, Robert Hurd himself. He carries the same torch, and his practice and his preaching have ensured that the tradition he champions lives on.

St Giles, the High Kirk, one-time cathedral, is more landmark than church for its compelling skyline crown which crops up from unlikely viewpoints all over Edinburgh. It is a brave, impressive bulk too, throwing a great shadow into the winter street, but ham-fisted restorations and cover-ups over the thousand years of its pre-eminence have not assisted the cause of spirituality here. But today's restorers seem more aware of what is at stake, and who can doubt that a thousand years from now St. Giles will still crown the best old man-made skyline in the land. And the Old Town of Edinburgh will look no older than it has always done.

THE CASTLE FROM SALISBURY CRAGS

Arguably the best viewpoint of all from which to appreciate the
relationship between the Castle and the Old Town is Salisbury Crags, where a steep
and wide cliff path climbs the west-facing flank of Arthur's Seat. The viewpoint
also reveals the precipitous depths of the 'back' of the Castle Rock.

THE PALACE OF HOLYROODHOUSE FROM SALISBURY CRAGS

Evening at 'Holyrood Palace', the low sunlight showing clearly
the difference of the centuries in its west-facing stonework. The more distant
of the two frontages is Mary Queen of Scots's tower house. It was simply
incorporated and its facade copied for the opposite wing
of the late seventeenth century palace.

COAT OF ARMS , PALACE OF HOLYROODHOUSE MAIN ENTRANCE

JOHN KNOX HOUSE, HIGH STREET

The most famous house in town is the mansion where
John Knox is reputed to have lived briefly, a 16th-century adaptation
of 15th-century origin. It is as charismatic as it is old, but a museum not an
inhabited house. Its timbered galleries were a hallmark
of the mediaeval street.

THE WAVERLEY, ST MARY'S STREET

Connoisseurs of good pubs are well served in Edinburgh,
particularly in the Old Town and the New Town. Restoration work
all over the city has spilled over into pub frontages. This imaginative treatment
in black and white is a well-known folk music haunt and landmark
just off the Royal Mile.

GREYFRIARS BOBBY

Edinburgh's most famous and best loved animal, immortalised
in book and film, now stands on his own plinth on George IV Bridge
near Greyfriars Churchyard. Bobby not only won the distinction of the Freedom
of Edinburgh, his reincarnation is also the smallest listed 'building' in
the city. Opposite: Grander, but no more famous listed
buildings punctuate this view to the Pentland Hills.

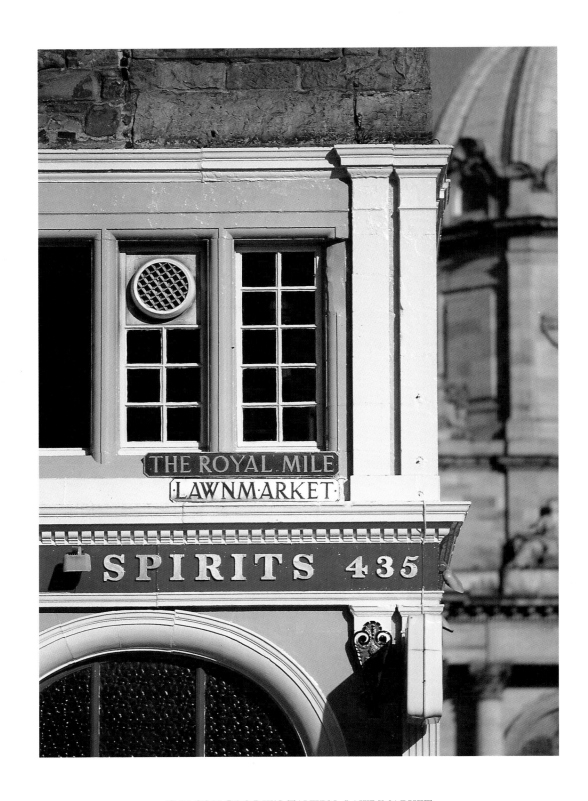

DEACON BRODIE'S TAVERN, LAWNMARKET

WARDROP'S COURT, LAWNMARKET

Many of the Royal Mile's closes reach under the street-facing
houses to hidden or half-hidden courtyards and mansions. Wardrop's
Court, with its mysterious dragon emblems, leads to the 17th-century tenement,
Blackie House. Some of the street's most intriguing architectural surprise
packages and most thoughtful restorations lie in such courtyards,
hidden from the passing throng.

GEORGE HERIOT'S SCHOOL

Victoria Terrace is the viewpoint for this study
of the uncompromising edifice of George Heriot's School. In the
foreground are the tenements of the Grassmarket, Victorian imitations of
the originals which rework the functional mediaeval invention
of crowstep gables as mere decoration.

VICTORIA STREET

Victoria Street is a vital street, swooping and curving
between George IV Bridge and the Grassmarket, well stocked
with fascinating and browseable shops, good eating places and watering
holes. The level Victoria Terrace cut into its tall flank is a greatly
underused space, but a fine south-facing viewpoint.

A MATCHLESS SKYLINE

The great crown spire of St Giles has adorned the matchless
Old Town skyline for so long that it often seems to act as a kind
of barometer-in-stone. On days like these it absorbs the early evening
mood of calm while it presides over its stored
legacy of history's storms.

THE NEW TOWN

No other Scottish city or town was ever handed the epoch-making opportunity that confronted Edinburgh in the mid-eighteenth century. The Old Town - all the Edinburgh there was then - was fearfully overpopulated, tenements collapsed and more were demolished, and Drummond was dreaming of bridges. The city was a poor capital and the wretched Treaty of Union of fifty years earlier had spirited the parliament away south. The city had not only to galvanise and expand, yet somehow to dignify itself at the same time, or at least such were Drummond's ambitions. The New Town would prove the ultimate solution, and although the germ of it was contained in 'The Proposals for carrying on certain Public Works in the City of Edinburgh' published in 1752, not even Drummond could have foreseen the scope and the scale of the showpiece he had spawned with his dreaming, nor that almost 250 years later it would be admired still, and cherished with a conservationist zeal unmatched elsewhere in urban Scotland.

A competition was finally announced (after a characteristic decade-and-a-half of bickering over money and other matters - very Edinburgh that) in 1766 and won by James Craig, an implausibly young and truculent architect whose sole claim to fame in an otherwise unremarkable career was to draw the meticulously elegant grid-iron shape of things to come.

It is curious to say the least, that an architect rated by posterity as one of stultifying mediocrity should be touched by one moment of genius. Ian Nimmo, a distinguished former editor of the Edinburgh Evening News, assesses the consequences of Craig's brainstorm in his refreshingly entertaining and thought-provoking book, 'Edinburgh - the New Town' (John Donald 1991):

> Nonetheless, by talent or luck, Craig's plan disciplined the growth of the New Town into a mould that at once gave it grandeur, grace, space, harmony. The concept of two large elegant squares - St Andrew Square and Charlotte Square - joined by the straight, wide and handsome thoroughfare of George Street, with less important streets running parallel and intersecting it, may not have been original, but when superimposed on Edinburgh's hilly contours Craig's imaginative use of space is immediately obvious and he should be given credit for it.

In addition, his two one-sided streets - Princes Street and Queen Street - designed to take best advantage of the dramatic hanging valley below the Castle and the serrated Old Town skyline to the south and the Fife vistas to the north again demonstrate an astute awareness of void as applied to the local terrain. It is claimed that the concept of streets with houses on one side (only half a street, claimed some detractors) was hardly new, and the pleasant city of Bath is indicated as an example of where it has worked well. But where is the effect put to better use than in the city of Edinburgh?

If you require proof of the excellence at work, an excellence dictated by the standard Craig set, consider the north side of Charlotte Square, where Robert Adam, arguably the best architect of his day, wrought a masterpiece. Today it accommodates the Secretary of State for Scotland, the Moderator of the General Assembly and the Georgian House headquarters of the National Trust for Scotland. In 1791, when work had reached the culminating stage of Craig's plan, recruiting Adam to its cause simply underscored Craig's - and Edinburgh's - declaration of intent. Adam, by now domiciled in London (he was a Scot, born in Kirkcaldy) and famed in European capitals, relished the opportunity to put his stamp on Edinburgh at such a pivotal point in its fortunes, and at the height of his powers. The result remains, and time has only mellowed the perfection of its execution. Adam added to his fame, and Edinburgh gained mightily in prestige.

It has all evolved, of course, and Princes Street, rather than George Street has become its celebrated thoroughfare, but few lovers of cityscapes can argue that the evolution has improved on the original. Princes Street is still stupendous, not for its shopping promenade which is a bit ordinary nor the 20th century architecture which is downright bad, but for the very thing Craig envisaged, its matchless contemplation of the Castle and the Old Town on the Rock. The valley of Princes Street Gardens is, in its own way, as remarkable a space for the heart of a modern city as Arthur's Seat. Not even the Victorian introduction of the railway through the bottom of the valley has inflicted any serious visual intrusion, and the aspect changes constantly in light and weather and season. Not that the railway didn't arouse outrage at the time. Lord Cockburn, a brilliant and far-sighted conservation pioneer raged at the demolition of the medieval Trinity College Church to make way for the railway: 'These people would remove Pompeii for a railway and tell us they had applied it to better use in Dundee!' Geddes condemned it thus: 'This railway

PRINCES STREET GARDENS

Few city centres anywhere can boast a more charming
open space with more dramatic views than Princes Street Gardens.
They were created on the site of the old Nor' Loch, occupying the valley between
the Old Town and Princes Street, first thoroughfare of the New Town.
Many natives like them best in leafless winter when mists and
flinty sunlight swathe the Old Town skyline.

THE OLD TOWN FROM THE NEW TOWN

Sunlight on the classical elegance and columns of the
New Town; shadow on the Old Town skyline . . . how often that
contrast stops you in your tracks as you wander through Edinburgh. The
spire is the Highland Tolbooth St John Kirk, the foreground
roof is the Royal Scottish Academy.

system . . . has been not merely half ruinous to the beauty of Edinburgh, but structurally bungled and economically wasteful to all concerned.' No matter, his Ramsay Garden is wonderfully seen from the Gardens and admired by thousands every year while the railway rumbles past below and unremarked.

Princes Street was the setting of another architectural competition, the one which put Edinburgh's second-most famous shortbread tin image on the face of the city's landscape, the one which built the Scott Monument. By Edinburgh's standards the thing was done with an astounding turn of speed, eight years from Scott's death in 1832 to the laying of the foundation stone in 1840. But as so often with architectural competitions in general and Edinburgh's in particular (and by 1840, remember, Edinburgh had become accustomed to such geniuses as Adam and Playfair toiling in their midst), the occasion was dogged by controversy bordering on uproar. The prize was fifty guineas, enough of a sum at the time to enthral Edinburgh's many architects and induce others from far beyond the city to try for a stake in the immortality which would surely follow the building of such a monument on such a stage as Princes Street. The architectural community held its breath, the winning design was unveiled and the winner's name pronounced: John Morvo. All that held breath now gushed out in a one-word response of incredulity. The word was: *'Who?'*

The controversy was hardly becalmed by the discovery that the Scott Monument was to be built by a pseudonym, for Morvo was in fact George Meikle Kemp, a shepherd's son, if you please, and (ye Gods!) an amateur! Why the organising committee and the competition's judges should have allowed themselves to be so lured into the storm of outrage which followed is not recorded, but the bald truth is that they had put one of the finest urban sites in the land at the disposal of an unknown unprofessional architect and permitted him to build a Gothic monster there. Edinburgh fairly hummed. Worse, 150 years after the event, it still does. It is no more certain what to do with the thing now than it was then. Should it be cleaned, or left as the blackened spire beloved of shortbread tins and Edinburgh Rock boxes? Some said that when it was encased in sheeted scaffolding for recent restoration work, it was a great improvement. A visiting Lord Provost suggested it should be painted white and was hastily ushered west again.

It has become, inevitably, a tourist whistlestop. Millions have climbed it and counted its 287 steps without ever reading a word of Scott that wasn't forced down their throats

NEW TOWN DOOR, INDIA STREET

by some dusty dominie. And perhaps the furore of 1840 and the legacy which the city has had to stomach ever since is why a protracted campaign for a monument to Stevenson has born no fruit. It is not that Edinburgh would not love to honour its greatest writer, just that it's terrified at the monster it might be lumbered with in his name.

Gardens are a good theme of the New Town, and any aerial photograph of the place is as notable for its well-nurtured greenery as for the curves and swoops and slashes of the buildings. The New Town grew, of course, far beyond the constraints of Craig's master plan, an orderly progress at first (Heriot Row, Great King Street and Fettes Row copied the Craig vision of one sided streets with a central spine), but then developed on a more piecemeal basis. Notwithstanding the decline in grandeur and grace as the city spilled downhill and northwards, the New Town is still a cohesive whole, true to the spirit if not the letter of Craig's ideal.

I think of it with particular fondness as an autumn place, the gardens vivid and fragrant with trailing blue drifts of smoke from heaps of fallen leaves, a paling, lowering sun on the rich shades of Craigleith sandstone (so admired in Adam's prime that it was shipped south for Buckingham Palace). To walk its streets on a still Sunday morning is to imbibe its unique sense of place, to acclimatise slowly to those first Georgian principles of space and form, classical elegance, uniformity laced with distinction (for even the uniformity of it is on a grand scale). It is a quiet time, the place barely roused at noon, the tumbling landscape of cliff and crag and sweep of hill barely concealed, the admiration growing for the manner in which its architects came to terms with what was tricky ground on which to build anything, never mind all Britain's finest showpiece of Georgian architecture.

Your eye reels from the far firth to a detail at your feet or on the wall in front of you. Stevenson lived idyllically happy here in Heriot Row. A plaque on the railings quotes from 'A Child's Garden of Verses' and you are at once grateful for the happy accident that surrounded the young genius with this of all Edinburgh landscapes. Years later, he would write of it from afar:

As the weather hardens towards frost, the world begins to improve for Edinburgh people. We enjoy superb, sub-arctic sunsets, with the profile of the city stamped in indigo upon a sky of luminous green. The wind may still be cold, but there is a briskness in the air that stirs the blood . . . One shivering evening, cold enough for frost but with too high a wind, and a little past sundown, when the lamps were beginning to enlarge their circles in the growing dusk, a brace of barefoot lassies were seen coming eastward in the teeth of the wind. If the one was as much as nine, the other was certainly not more than seven. They were miserably clad; and the pavement was so cold, you would have thought no one could lay a naked foot on it unflinching. Yet they came along waltzing, if you please, while the elder sang a tune to give them music. The person who saw this, and whose heart was full of bitterness at the moment, pocketed a reproof which has been of use to him ever since, and which he now hands on, with his good wishes, to the reader.

A late-in-the-year walk through the New Town never fails to reawaken that image in my mind, and although the lassies no longer go barefoot or miserably clad, you can wander the streets glimpsing great rooms or bonny basements the way a lassie of seven or nine might ponder the rooms of some fantastical doll's house. Moray Place is perhaps the most fantastical pause on such a walk, perfectly encircling its own secret garden, Adam-esque in its proportions and tone (although the architect was Gillespie Graham). Here, sleek and leisured cats curl watchfully on vast doorsteps. The New Town has come a long way by the time you have reached Moray Place, or the lowlier cloisterish fringes of Northumberland Street or Cumberland Street, and it has drifted far from Craig's centrepiece, but it never loses its sense of style or place. As Ian Nimmo puts it:

> James Craig and Robert Adam had put their stamp on Edinburgh for ever. They set the standards of the New Town and in so doing issued a challenge to others who would follow to do better if they could. Thankfully, there were many fine architects to succeed Adam and continue to create Edinburgh's fair face. Yet it is unlikely that there will ever be anything quite on the same scale or of such importance as the original building of the New Town. In perspective, the New Town and the ancient Old Town together make Edinburgh one of the most dramatic and beautiful capital cities in the world.

George Drummond, slumbrous in the cool Canongate earth, it was a good dream you dreamed.

SPRING IN CHARLOTTE SQUARE

NEW TOWN FRONTAGE, CASTLE STREET

INDIA STREET

The New Town has grown out far beyond the original
master plan produced by James Craig. India Street is typical of the ingenious
solutions to the very difficult terrain which later New Town architects
had to deal with as development moved northwards.

PRINCES STREET

The twentieth century has imposed many
changes on Princes Street, and little remains now
of the street as James Craig envisaged it. The most recent
buildings have rarely lived up to the standards of his ideals and
those of the early New Town architects. Yet still the street
retains the aura which derives from its
unique landscape setting.

CAFE ROYAL, WEST REGISTER STREET

The Cafe Royal tucked away behind Princes Street's east
end is a beautifully appointed building with tiled murals, stained glass
windows, marble floor and huge Circle Bar. Incredible as it seems now, it was
threatened with demolition as recently as 1969, during an era in which
Edinburgh acquired some of its least appropriate buildings.

KAY'S BAR, JAMAICA STREET

THE LAST OF THE MILK HORSES

His name was Trigger, and he pulled the St Cuthbert's
Dairy milk cart until a few years ago. The St Cuthbert's horses were
the last to be used in Britain, and they are still much missed by Edinburgh people
of all ages. The sight and the sound - and the smell - of them is unforgettable,
and the city's roses have never been the same.

THE ROYAL SCOTTISH ACADEMY

Architects of the stature of William Playfair made sure
that their buildings had no unflattering 'backs' to them as this rear
view of the Royal Scottish Academy from the Mound demonstrates. During the
Edinburgh Festival his noble columns and steps play host to tides
of strolling players and buskers.

SUNLIGHT ON STEEL BELOW PRINCES STREET GARDENS

THE CASTLE AND THE ROCK

The last few steps up the narrowing and introverting gloom of Castlehill impart a strange tension on any thinking explorer of Edinburgh. You know the Castle is ahead, but it is well nigh invisible until you iron out the last little kink in the Royal Mile. It should, you might reason, be the only logical conclusion to the crown of the city, the Castle in all its fabled splendour, the no-contest superstar of the place. Then your eye is caught by the thunder-stealer, wonder of wonders, Ramsay Garden.

If you are new to the Royal Mile, Ramsay Garden is an astonishment, clinging improbably to its cliff as tenacious as a colony of kittiwakes, tall columns of white and red houses carefully planned into a climbing joyous confusion of north-facing rooftop shapes, as unlike the rest of Old Town Edinburgh as anything tall and stone-built could be. It is the one place in the entire street which you might call truly beautiful. It is also outrageous, preposterously romantic and inspired, the stroke of a very daring genius. It was Patrick Geddes at work, practising what he had preached for years about inducing a resurrection of spirit into the then tawdry Old Town. He wanted to enhance the social mix, and hoped to lure back to the Royal Mile some of the social classes which had long since emigrated to the New Town, people like university professors, for example. Geddes chose the one-time home of poet Allan Ramsay for his centrepiece, a deliciously quirky octagonal house which left him free to cluster every conceivable house shape around it and above it. Ramsay Garden was something of a turning point in the Royal Mile's fortunes too, for Geddes had shown how it might blossom again under appropriate reforming zeal. That zeal, through such architects as Hurd and Begg, has gathered pace through the twentieth century, although there can only ever be one Ramsay Garden, just as there can only ever be one Edinburgh Castle.

The Castle is a book in itself, a series of books, a small library of books if you would detail the lives of those who have strutted its stage, and forged and fouled their destinies here. It remains a place of awesome power, a Mons Meg of a Castle. An information board in the vaults articulates its significance in the sixteenth century thus:

The Castle then stood at the summit of its pre-eminence: fortress, palace, arsenal, treasury, state prison and repository of the national archives: it was the chief place of ceremony in the kingdom where great banquets and state assemblies, including Parliament, were held.

From primitive fortress to the all-purpose hub of a nation; it is a singular progress and a singular story. Today its buildings range from the languishing sunless vaults to the tiny, simple and endearing chamber of St Margaret's Chapel, to Sir Robert Lorimer's overwhelming Scottish National War Museum for the First World War. Its military archive is stupendous, its history matchless, its presence matched only, perhaps, by Stirling Castle, forty miles upriver. Its essence for me distils, however clumsily, and inadequately into a threefold symbolic response.

The first is to confront and marvel at Mons Meg, the cannon. To throw her adjectives like 'great' or 'mighty' is to belittle the beast. To have her on your side in her heyday was to win. Her? A piece of artillery with a personality? You must go and stand and stare and judge for yourself. Cromwell did not doubt it, for one. His inventory of captured guns lists 'the great iron murderer, Meg'. Sir Walter Scott rescued her from ignominy in the Tower of London, and brought her home with an escort, from Leith, of three troops of cavalry and a pipe band. How often has such a tribute been accorded to an obsolete gun? She thrives now in her role as superstar in retirement, the more tourist bustle about her the more blatant her contemptuous aloofness. She did it all. She exerts the kind of influence hereabouts that Mary has won in Holyrood, heroines both who lived in daring times and were not found wanting. She fired a salute for Mary's first wedding. The missile travelled two miles.

My second response is altogether more solemn, more private, more idealistic, more romantic, more nationalistic. It is to ponder might-have-beens in the gilded and pearled company of Scottish Regalia. The crown room is a place to come upon in one of the Castle's quieter hours because it symbolises that which is lost, which all Scots - and many non-Scots - hold deep and dear. Some will qualify the degree to which they will admit to the sentiment of loss, but none can deny the instinct.

I am not the first to be moved by the encased symbolism of the Scottish Regalia. It was Scott again whose steadfast patriotism won them back for their home and their people. Like much else which was subdued by the Treaty of Union, the Regalia suffered concealment, on the basis that out of sight was out of the minds of the disapproving mob.

TOWARDS THE CASTLE FROM NORTH BRIDGE

EDINBURGH CASTLE GATEHOUSE

George IV finally responded to Sir Walter's campaign in 1817 and ordered the Crown Room to be unlocked after twenty-three years to ascertain whether the Regalia still existed, or whether, as many had begun to believe, they had been removed to England. It was a sweet moment for Sir Walter Scott and Scotland. None of Scott's invented plots ever held higher drama than that single climactic moment. He wrote it thus:

It was with feelings of no common anxiety that the commissioners having read their warrant, proceeded to the crown-room, and having found all there in the state in which it had been left in 1794, the last time the room had been opened, during a search for lost Parliamentary records, commanded the King's Smith, who was in attendance, to force open the great chest, the keys of which had been sought for in vain. The general impression that the Regalia had been secretly removed weighed heavily on the hearts of all while the labour proceeded. The chest seemed to return a hollow and empty sound to the strokes of the hammer; and even those whose expectations had been most sanguine felt at that moment the probability of disappointment, and could not but be sensible that, should the result of the search confirm those forebodings, it would only serve to show that a national affront - an injury had been sustained, for which it might be difficult, or rather impossible, to obtain redress. The joy was therefore extreme when, the ponderous lid of the chest having been forced open, at the expense of some time and labour, the Regalia were discovered lying at the bottom covered with linen cloths, exactly as they had been left in 1707, being 110 years before, since they had been surrendered by William the ninth Earl Marischal to the custody of the Earl of Glasgow, Treasurer-Deputy of Scotland. The reliques were passed from hand to hand, and greeted with the affectionate reverence which emblems so venerable, restored to public view after a slumber of more than a hundred years, were so peculiarly calculated to excite. The discovery was instantly communicated to the public by the display of the Royal Standard, and was greeted by shouts of the soldiers in the garrison and a vast multitude assembled on the Castle hill; indeed the rejoicing was so general and sincere as plainly to show that, however altered in other respects, the people of Scotland had lost nothing of that national enthusiasm which formerly had displayed itself in grief for the loss of those emblematic honours, and now was expressed in joy for their recovery.

My third distillation of the essence of Edinburgh Castle is to make the small pilgrimage to St Margaret's Chapel. St Margaret was the English wife of Malcolm Canmore, one of Scotland's more warlike Kings, and a constant harrier of England's northmost airts. But although Margaret would have felt more at home in a nunnery than in Royal splendour, she was a woman of enlightenment, and as compassionate as she was learned. Her husband's greatest saving grace was that he doted on her and marvelled at her sophistication and her determined reformation of what she considered to be the crudeness of the Celtic church. But Malcolm Canmore was not alone in his adoration of Margaret, for thousands of poor commoners had cause to be grateful for her charitable works. She went among them constantly, distributing her own riches and often those of the King too. Legend has it that the King once saw her kneel to wash the feet of some ragged wretch of a beggar and was so moved by her actions that he at once knelt beside her. That a beggar should have his feet washed by his King and Queen at once is one of Scottish history's less likely moments, but there are those who swear it happened, and it is nothing if not in keeping with spirit and the reputation of St Margaret. Her Chapel is the oldest intact building in the Castle.

Many people who come to the Royal Mile today will prefer to walk down it rather than climb it, because it is easier. This approach denies, however, the perspective which falls into place with the attainment of this rough and ready wind-washed end. Within, it is a subtle place, white and subtle and simple - pure, I think - set with small, vivid stained glass windows, and the perpetual flowers which uphold a good tradition. It is that each week, a woman called Margaret, a member of the St Margaret Chapel Guild, puts flowers in the chapel.

It is as simple and appropriate as that. It is a commemoration of a quite remarkable familiarity, as though she had died a year ago, rather than 900 years. Ronald Selby Wright writes in the chapel booklet: '. . . will you come in imagination out of the world into a few minutes of God's peace, and go back again to whatever work you have to do, renewed and refreshed, feeling that it was good to have been there'. The booklet's 21st reprint in 1984 denoted 1,250,000 copies since the first printing in 1957. Queen Margaret, the saint, wins hearts and minds still, and it does not matter what manner of God you hold to . . . it will have been good to be there.

RAMSAY GARDEN FROM PRINCES STREET GARDENS

Ramsay Garden was perhaps the greatest of Patrick Geddes'
many contributions to the Edinburgh landscape. Its red and white
turn-of-the-century architecture is unlike anything else in the city and adds
a rousing finale to the Royal Mile as it enters the Castle Esplanade.
The gaunt spire is the Highland Tolbooth St John Kirk.

THE ASSEMBLY HALL AND THE MOUND CHRISTMAS TREE

THE FORTRESS ON THE ROCK

The strategic value of Edinburgh Castle as a defendable
fortress is self-evident even today. The Castle Rock is a volcanic plug
with a glacial tail dwindling downhill to the east. The clifftop nature of the
fortress site itself made it all but impregnable, and the glacial tail
was the perfect setting for the first walled town. It was here,
unknown millenia ago, that Edinburgh began.

RAMSAY GARDEN IN SPRING

The full unfettered scope of the architectural wizardry
deployed by Patrick Geddes in this unique collection of houses
is well seen here. The rooftop reds are at their warmest and the contrast
with the gray slate roofs is particularly marked. The winterscape
opposite pales the whole mass and confers briefly a
completely new magic for which not even
Geddes can take credit.

RAMSAY GARDEN IN WINTER

NORTH BRIDGE AND THE CASTLE

THE CASTLE FROM THE GRASSMARKET

The Castle is a particularly forbidding presence from the
Grassmarket, but then the Grassmarket of old was not without a
forbidding presence of its own. Its enclosed and set aside
nature still conveys an introspective air.

RAMSAY GARDEN FROM THE CASTLE ESPLANADE

The top of Ramsay Garden rises close at hand above a
north-facing corner of the Castle Esplanade, a startling and welcome
intrusion of bright colour after the last few dark yards of Castlehill. It does not
matter how you come on Ramsay Garden, the miracle of it never fails.
Opposite: The Firth of Forth and Berwick Law from the Castle.

THE LIVING CITY

Edinburgh may be old but it is no museum piece. It lives. It breathes, evolves, redevelops, conserves. Its set pieces and showpieces may look as old as the Pentland Hills, but they are also the built fabric of a modern city. Edinburgh's city centre is *lived* in, a fact which is in itself something of a rarity. As recently as the 1960s, the Old Town had fallen on another of its hard times, but the last two decades have witnessed a spectacular revival of its fortunes and its population is once again healthy and rising , and restorations and rebuildings have put a twentieth century spring in its old mediaeval step. Such transformations do not happen by accident. A new generation of councillors and council officials (often a much maligned tribe in this most political of cities) have shown an awareness of the city's sense of place in their reformist zeal, and it is a subtle stamp they have put on the city.

Change in Edinburgh should always be subtle, solution rather than revolution, for its characteristic distinguishing (and distinguished) elements have been in place for centuries. They cannot be improved upon, and thoughtful development will always defer to them. The perpetual challenge facing Edinburgh's administrators will always be to fit the fabric of a modern capital city into a matchless framework. It is fair to say that that task is being handled as well today as it has ever been.

The Scandic Crown Hotel in the Royal Mile is a perfect example of a rare development opportunity in the city's mediaeval heart handled with daring discretion. The Scottish Financial Centre in Castle Terrace is another solution to an intractable dilemma which had bedevilled the city for the best part of thirty years. It is arguable now - but only now that the solution is found and found to be graceful - that in the history of the Edinburgh landscape, thirty years is but a blink and it was worth the wait. It works because it complements the cityscape, down to the curve of the facade which honours the curve of the street and contemplates the Castle Rock at its craggiest. Its completion and its success reflect an enabling and invigorating climate in the city which has begun to believe in itself again (publicly, that is, for privately, the people of Edinburgh have a calm pride in their city which is unshakeable) and begun to achieve again.

If any one building characterises that mood, it is what used to be affectionately called the NB - the North British Hotel. That great blackened and crumpled cube with its corner clock tower was as emblematic of Edinburgh and Princes Street as the Scott Monument, but ten years ago it had become no-one's idea of a top class hotel. After a change or two of ownership and a grand design or two unfulfilled, it succumbed to the great Edinburgh stone-cleaning controversy, and to far from muted protest it vanished behind screens of scaffolding. You might as well paint the Castle Rock white. But when it emerged butterfly-bold and floodlit from its clamorous chrysalis, and with Drummond's dream bridge to the Old Town newly a-glitter with vivid paint and floodlighting, even Edinburgh's hardiest sceptics wilted. Hardly anyone noticed that the NB had acquired an extra storey, and hardly anyone still remembers that the very existence of the building contravenes Craig's New Town blueprint. There were to be no buildings on the south side of Princes Street, and nothing should rise above street level. But lots of things about the NB go unnoticed, whether by accident or design, and not the least of these is that when it changed its name to the Balmoral to honour its new guise, most of Edinburgh still went right on calling it the NB. It will never be a beautiful building, nor even an architecturally significant one, but Edinburgh holds its conspicuous solidity in great affection.

I have mixed feelings about it. I subscribe to the view of one noted Edinburgh conservationist who suggested that in addition to the A,B, and C listings for architectural merit, there should also be an X category, into which the NB would fall. The category denotes a building which should be cared for while it stood because of a certain eccentric or landmark quality, but would not be exempt from demolition. For what it's worth, I would put the Scott Monument in the same category, although I find a worthy exception to Craig's rule in Playfair's galleries along the street.

The National Gallery of Scotland and the Royal Scottish Academy are more than just treasure stores of great works of art. They are great works themselves, and because they stand where they do, and because they are as accommodating to people on their outside walls as they are to artworks inside, they have become a part of another unique aspect of Edinburgh. For Edinburgh is a theatre, and its great works are a stage set unlike any other in the world. It is to this theatre that the Edinburgh International Festival is lured for three weeks every summer, and a dozen lesser festivals in various seasons. The Edinburgh Festival and its Fringe have become almost embarrassed by success. It is generally agreed now that they have become *too* big, appropriated *too* much of essential

THE ROYAL BOTANIC GARDENS

THE ROYAL MUSEUM OF SCOTLAND

Edinburgh for their own uses, but there are few qualms about the way they have spilled into the streets and into the square around the galleries in particular. There is a whole festival-for-free for much of the day and night amid Playfair's benevolent shadows. An avenue of buskers and stalls and shifting tides of performers and audiences make a carnival of the place. The theatre is also as unforgettable a part of the Festival's now traditional fireworks concert as the fireworks themselves. Many cities have looked enviously at Edinburgh's Festival, and sought to copy it or even steal it, but the one thing no city can replicate is the one thing that sets the Edinburgh Festival apart from all others: Edinburgh itself, the star of its own show.

And when the Festival bandwagon rolls out of town and the place tidies up and empties and quietens again, it becomes again the Edinburgh the rest of us take to our hearts again, and again, year after year, Festival after Festival, for by then it stands on the brink of a new autumn, and it will be time to go quietly through our New Town Sundays, hearing our own footfall again and scenting the leaf-smoke, and there will be no city on earth quite like it.

Edinburgh is a wider city than this book has indicated, of course, for it flows from the foot of the Pentland Hills to the Firth of Forth, and there is hardly a dull acre in between. There are outlying beauties like the Botanic Gardens (yet even there the Castle crops up, far off, the way you glimpse the Cuillin from some northern outpost of Skye); there are great commercial excitements (if you are excited by commercial doings) like the so-called new New Town west of Lothian Road. Time will tell if its un-Edinburgh buildings will lay any kind of claim to posterity or rather just to passing fancy, but it is being boldly done. Further west still, and more boldly still, Edinburgh has given vent to a Titanic commercial urge, building vast American-style cathedrals to consumerism on the city boundary. By no stretch of the imagination can what has been built lay claim to anything which is distinctively Edinburgh, although it is arguable that there will be profound consequences for the evolution of the city centre. The abdication of what were once city centre names all over the country to retail parks on the edge of cities all over the country are rarely viewed as optimistic portents for the wellbeing of the civic heartbeat. But Edinburgh does not conform to the rules of lesser cities. Its heart is unique, and whether or not the retail trade will always want to maintain a presence there, people will always want to live there. Perhaps, for example, Princes Street will grow so unfashionable as a shopping street that

Edinburgh will recognise an opportunity for it to revert to the residential one-sided masterstroke which James Craig conceived. Perhaps then, it would be time for Edinburgh to devise one more architectural competition. Perhaps, even now, a new Craig is sharpening his embryonic genius unaware of the immortality which awaits. Perhaps he will honour his famous predecessor and insist on sweeping away the NB and the Scott Monument, the unloved Waverley Market and an unremarkable clutter at the street's West End corner; perhaps he will insist on higher standards for the Gardens redefining the valley, burying the railway. If he does, he will have my vote.

Yet in all this store of greatness - architectural, artistic, historical, even natural - there is a missing piece in the complex and ancient jigsaw which is Edinburgh. It is the one which was spirited away to London on January 16, 1707 when the Scottish Parliament finally put its reluctant signature on the Treaty of Union, and by doing so ceased to exist. Scotland-wide outrage greeted the deed, and the signatories had to flee an inconsolable mob which chased them down the Royal Mile until they found ignominious refuge in a summer house in the garden of Moray House. There, in surroundings which could not be construed as other than an ill omen, the deed was done.

As I write, there is a permanent vigil in place at the foot of the Calton Hill directly across from St Andrew's House and near the empty Royal High School building which would have housed the new Scottish Parliament after devolution in 1979, that devolution which never happened. The vigil is a pointed reminder. The case for a Scottish Parliament is an urgent argument again, and Edinburgh is at the centre of the argument. In truth, it has never really stood anywhere else.

The argument can be as party-political or as apolitical as you want it to be, but in the context of this book, it is simply one more piece of the fabric of Edinburgh, a piece of its story, but it is a fundamental piece and central to the city's very existence. There is a world of difference between a city only nominally capital of a Scotland which is only nominally a nation, and the social, economic, cultural and instinctive pride of a true capital city host to its country's Parliament. That Parliament must conduct as many of its country's affairs as its people would like it to, so whether the Parliament be devolved or independent, Edinburgh will be less of a city than it should be - or than it has been - until the vigil on Calton Hill dowses its brazier and the flame of a Scottish Parliament is rekindled.

FIREWORKS CONCERT

The Glenlivet Fireworks Concerts have become something of a
modern tradition as a show-stopper of the official Edinburgh International
Festival. It is, perhaps more than any of the other Festival event, the one
in which Edinburgh comes into its own as a supreme stage set.

THE TWO FACES OF THE BALMORAL

Edinburgh has known two faces of the Balmoral Hotel.
Above is the modern one, stone-cleaned and floodlit, which it
is slowly coming to terms with. Opposite is the one many still hanker for,
the blackened bulk of the North British Hotel which always seemed
so much more of an Edinburgh landmark. In Edinburgh of all
places, beauty is very much the preserve of the beholder.

THE COLONIES, ABBEYHILL

Edinburgh has several developments of colonies housing.
They were built in the second half of last century by cooperative
building societies to provide houses for working-class owner-occupiers,
selling for around £200 each. Two storeys and outside
stairs are characteristic.

NEW TOWN DOORSTEP
The uniformity with which whole New Town streets must
comply has not stifled ingenuity where floral decoration is concerned.
Doorstep tubs like these, creepers on railings, and startling hidden gardens
outside basement doors abound to delight the eye of
the passing pedestrian.

THE FORTH RAILWAY BRIDGE

The vast cantilevered bulk of the Forth Railway Bridge is
simply one of the most famous engineering feats in the world and
probably the single most famous structural shape in Scotland. In recent years
floodlighting has added to its fame and greatly increased
its attraction for visitors.

SHOP FRONT, WEST NICHOLSON STREET

SHOP DOORWAY, ST MARY'S STREET

CANONGATE KIRK

The stag's head and the cross commemorate a legendary
incident in which the life of King David I was saved after he had
fallen from his horse while hunting. He was at the mercy of a stag until the
vision of a cross appeared between its antlers and it fled. In his
gratitude, the King built Holyrood Abbey.

'SOME SUNSET BEHIND THE CASTLE CLIFFS'
Robert Louis Stevenson wrote: 'There is no Edinburgh
emigrant, far or near, from China to Peru, but he or she carries some
lively pictures in the mind, some sunset behind the Castle cliffs, some snow
scene, some maze of city lamps, indelible to the memory and
delightful to study in the intervals of toil . . .'

INDEX OF PHOTOGRAPHS